Brands We Know

Kraft

By Sara Green

Bellwether Media • Minneapolis, MN

Jump into the cockpit and take flight with Pilot books. Your journey will take you on high-energy adventures as you learn about all that is wild, weird, fascinating, and fun!

This edition first published in 2017 by Bellwether Media, Inc.

Library of Congress Cataloging-in-Publication Data

Names: Green, Sara, 1964- author.
Title: Kraft / by Sara Green.
Description: Minneapolis, MN : Bellwether Media, Inc., 2017. | Series:
 Pilot. Brands We Know | Includes bibliographical references and index.
|Audience: Age 7-13.
Identifiers: LCCN 2015049958 | ISBN 9781626174092 (hardcover : alk.
paper)
Subjects: LCSH: Kraft Heinz Company--History--Juvenile literature. |
Food industry and trade--United States--History--Juvenile literature. |
Kraft, James Lewis, 1874-1953--Juvenile literature.
Classification: LCC HD9009.K73 G74 2017 | DDC 338.7/66400973--dc23
LC record available at http://lccn.loc.gov/2015049958

Printed in the United States of America, North Mankato, MN.

Table of Contents

What Is Kraft?

Dinner is ready. The kids smile when they see what is on the table. Macaroni & Cheese from the Blue Box! It is a favorite food. Salad with Velveeta Cheesy Ranch dressing is also served. For dessert, the family enjoys Creamy Layered Squares. These are made with Philadelphia Cream Cheese, Jell-O, and Cool Whip. All these **brands** come from Kraft!

Kraft is part of a larger company called Kraft Heinz. The company is built from many brands and **founders**. Its two **headquarters** are in Chicago, Illinois, and Pittsburgh, Pennsylvania. Kraft Heinz is the fifth-largest food and **beverage** company in the world. People across the globe recognize the company's many brands. These include Oscar Mayer, Planters, and Kool-Aid. The company produces some of the most famous food brands on Earth!

By the Numbers

more than
$27 billion
total sales in 2015

around
200
countries that sell Kraft
Heinz products

5th
largest food and
beverage company
in the world

45
countries with Kraft
Heinz employees

8
Kraft Heinz brands
worth more than
$1 billion

more than
200
Kraft Heinz
brands

KRAFT

Kraft factory, Pennsylvania

A Cheesy History

James Lewis, or J.L., Kraft is the father of the Kraft brand. J.L. grew up on a dairy farm in Ontario, Canada. In 1903, he moved to Chicago, Illinois, with $65. J.L. rented a wagon and a horse named Paddy. He decided to start a cheese delivery service. He bought large wheels of cheese from **warehouses** every morning. He sliced the cheese and wrapped it in foil. Then, he resold the slices to local stores.

J.L. Kraft

Because of the exclusive Kraft process of sterilizing, Elkhorn Cheese in Tins is always uniform and always good. Stock up now.

J. L. KRAFT & BROS. CO.
NEW YORK   CHICAGO

If your dealer does not have Elkhorn Cheese in Tins, send his name and 10c in stamps or coin for sample tin of Kraft plain or Pimento flavor, or 20c for both. Illustrated book of recipes free. Address 361-3 River St., Chicago, Illinois.

ELKHORN
TRADE MARK   REG. U. S. PAT. OFF.
KRAFT CHEESE
CONTENTS   7¾ OUNCES
STERILIZED
AMERICAN CHEDDAR

J.L. struggled to earn money at first. But he believed in his idea and continued to work hard. Eventually, more people bought his cheese. He was then able to expand his business. In 1909, J.L.'s brothers joined him. It was time to give the company a name. They called it J.L. Kraft & Bros. Co. Soon, the company was selling 31 types of cheese. Cheddar was the most popular!

Refrigerators were uncommon during the early 1900s. Cheese spoiled easily. J.L. dreamed of cheese that stayed fresh longer and was easy to package. In 1915, he found a way to blend and **pasteurize** cheese. This gave it a longer **shelf life**. He received a **patent** for his process the next year. He also began packaging the cheese in small tins.

Cheese is Kraft

Kraft Singles 1960s tagline

Cheese Overseas
During World War I, Kraft sent more than 6 million pounds (2.7 million kilograms) of processed cheese to troops overseas.

Spoon it

KRAFT

KRAFT'S
Cheez Whiz
For Fast Cheese Treats
A PASTEURIZED PROCESS CHEESE SPREAD

MELTS ON HOT FOODS
...instantly!

PACIFIC OUTDOOR

FREE
RECIPES
at grocers

PHILADELPHIA BRAND CREAM CHEESE

PACIFIC OUTDOOR

In 1928, J.L. joined his company with the Phenix Cheese Company. This was the maker of Philadelphia Cream Cheese. Within ten years, the company introduced Miracle Whip Dressing and Kraft's Macaroni & Cheese Dinner. The company had also moved into Canada, Europe, and Australia. By the late 1960s, Kraft made many other products. Cheez Whiz, Cool Whip, and Kraft Singles became popular.

J.L. believed in the power of **advertising**. His first ads ran in newspapers and grocery store fliers. In 1919, Kraft began posting ads in magazines. In time, Kraft became a **sponsor** of a radio show called *Kraft Music Hall*. A television show called *Kraft Television Theatre* came out in 1947. Its popular commercials showed a pair of hands cooking with Kraft products. The recipes were created by a woman named Marye Dahnke.

For nearly 40 years, Marye helped bring Kraft products into people's kitchens. She first found work with Kraft Cheese Company in 1925. She handed out cheese samples at stores. The next year, she traveled the country to teach people different ways to use cheese. In time, Marye became director of Kraft's Consumer Service Department. Her role at Kraft helped increase cheese **consumption** nationwide.

Bing Crosby recording
Kraft Music Hall

A Meal for 4... in 9 Minutes
Kraft Macaroni & Cheese Dinner 1930s tagline

Classic Cookbooks
Marye Dahnke published *The Cheese Cook Book* and *Marye Dahnke's Salad Book* in the 1950s.

KRAFT
De Luxe
SLICES
8 SLICES
PASTEURIZED PROCESS
AMERICAN CHEESE

AMERICAN
PIMENTO
BRICK
SWISS
OLD ENGLISH

"Easy as peeling a banana..."

Growth and Change

Over time, Kraft continued to grow. The company joined with General Foods Corporation in 1989. This company was founded by Charles William, or C.W., Post in 1895. With General Foods, the Kraft family grew to include the Oscar Mayer, Kool-Aid, and Jell-O brands. Kraft **merged** again in 2000. Nabisco became a part of the company. Adolphus Green and William Moore founded Nabisco. It is famous for Oreo Cookies and Ritz Crackers.

Kraft's huge food company was a success. But its large size made management difficult. Kraft leaders had to find an easier way to run it. In 2012, they split Kraft into two different companies. This gave each company more freedom and space to grow. One company became Kraft Foods Group. It took charge of products sold in North America. The other is Mondelēz **International**. It is in charge of Newtons, Cadbury, and other snacks sold around the world.

A Cool Drink

A man named Edwin Perkins invented Kool-Aid in the 1920s. It first came as a syrup called Fruit Smack. Powder packets of Kool-Aid hit stores in 1927.

Remember how much you loved Kool-Aid® as a kid?

Now you love it as a mother.

Kool-Aid

SOFT DRINK MIX   BRAND

13

In 2015, Kraft Foods Group became Kraft Heinz. It merged with a food company called H.J. Heinz. The Heinz company was founded by Henry John Heinz in 1869. Henry believed in patience and fairness. He kept his factories clean and made sure working conditions were safe. People came to trust the Heinz name. The brand is now more than 140 years old! Today, Kraft Heinz is the third-largest food and beverage company in North America.

Kraft Heinz has more than 200 different brands, including Lunchables, Classico, and Miracle Whip. It also has international brands. Many people eat packaged Wattie's foods in New Zealand. Brinta hot cereal and bread are popular breakfast items in the Netherlands.

Henry John Heinz

Ketchup King
More than 650 million bottles of Heinz Ketchup are sold around the world each year!

HEINZ
57 VARIETIES

HEINZ
est 1869
TOMATO KETCHUP
57 VARIETIES

℮342g

Famous Kraft Heinz Brands

Brand Name	Known For
A.1.	steak sauce
Capri Sun	juice pouches
Classico	pasta sauce
Claussen	pickles
Cool Whip	whipped topping
Heinz	ketchup
Jell-O	gelatin
Jet-Puffed	marshmallows
Kool-Aid	juice mix
Kraft Singles	sliced cheese
Lunchables	packaged lunches
Maxwell House	coffee
Miracle Whip	dressing
Oscar Mayer	hot dogs

Fun and Healthy Food

Many families enjoy **classic** Kraft products. These include Kraft Singles and Natural Cheese. However, Kraft continues to develop new foods and flavors. Macaroni noodles are shaped like Minions or SpongeBob characters. This makes Kraft Macaroni & Cheese Dinners fun to eat. Recently, Kraft came out with a new barbecue sauce recipe. It is called Kraft Hot & Spicy.

So Cheesy!
The original flavor of Kraft's Macaroni & Cheese is called The Cheesiest. Cheesasaurus Rex helped promote the product in the 2000s.

You know you love it.

Kraft Macaroni & Cheese 2010s tagline

Kraft also offers healthier food choices. The company added **whole grains** and **nutrients** to many of its foods. Kraft has more options for its cheeses and salad dressings. Jell-O, Capri Sun, and other products may have little or no sugar. Products can also be low-fat or fat-free. Oscar Mayer bacon and smoked ham have less salt than earlier versions. Oscar Mayer also came out with a healthy snack called P3. It often includes cheese, meat, and nuts.

A Caring Company

Kraft gives back in many ways. Over time, the company has given more than 2 billion servings of food to organizations that fight hunger. In addition, a large fruit and vegetable garden grows outside of the Chicago headquarters. Many Kraft employees plant and harvest the garden. The fresh **produce** goes to **food pantries** and soup kitchens.

The company has also given more than $14 million to the American Red Cross since 2000. The money is often put toward food, water, and shelter. This helps people in areas hit by **hurricanes** and other disasters.

Company **volunteers** also make a difference. Every April during Make an Impact, Kraft encourages volunteer service. Kraft employees have volunteered in more than 470 community projects since 2013. Some volunteers help teach kids how to live healthy. Others sort and pack food that will be given away to those in need. Kraft and its employees fill hearts and stomachs each day!

. . . .

Stop Hunger Now

Kraft Heinz partners with Stop Hunger Now in India. Vans deliver milk and other nutrients to areas in need.

Kraft donations after Hurricane Sandy

Kraft Timeline

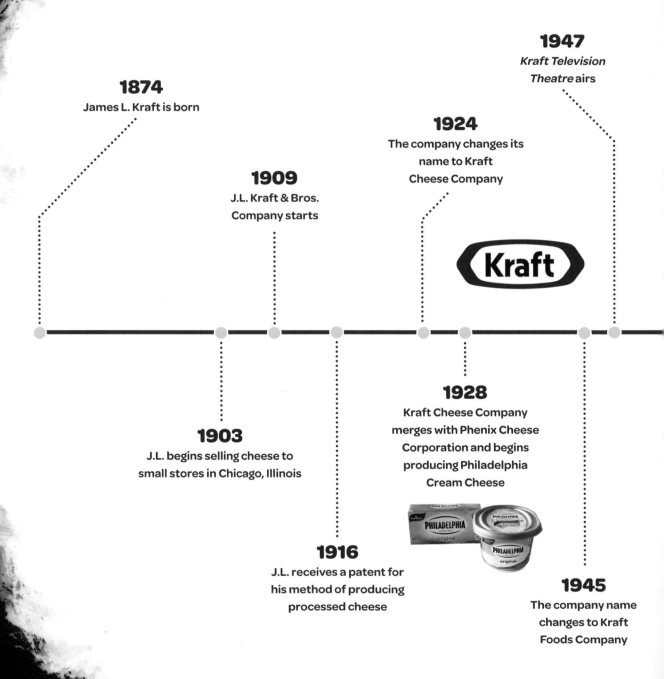

1874
James L. Kraft is born

1909
J.L. Kraft & Bros. Company starts

1924
The company changes its name to Kraft Cheese Company

1947
Kraft Television Theatre airs

1903
J.L. begins selling cheese to small stores in Chicago, Illinois

1928
Kraft Cheese Company merges with Phenix Cheese Corporation and begins producing Philadelphia Cream Cheese

1916
J.L. receives a patent for his method of producing processed cheese

1945
The company name changes to Kraft Foods Company

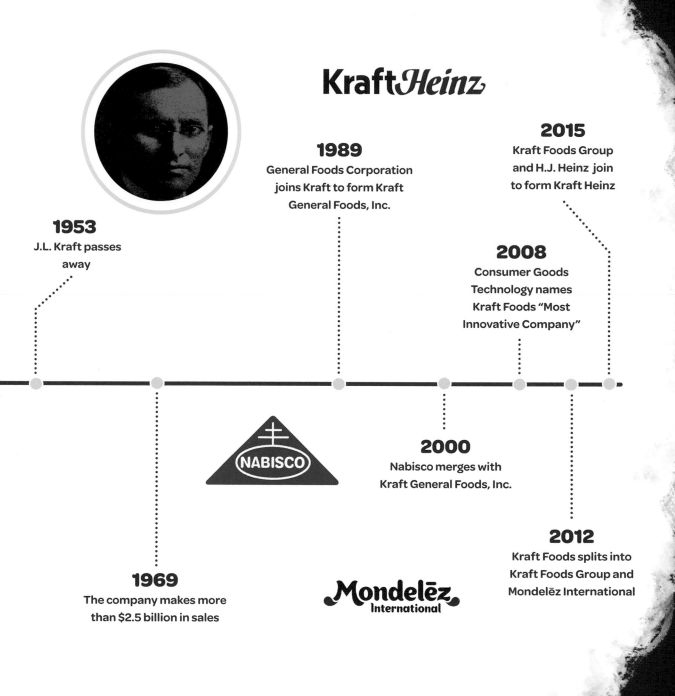

KraftHeinz

1953
J.L. Kraft passes away

1989
General Foods Corporation joins Kraft to form Kraft General Foods, Inc.

2015
Kraft Foods Group and H.J. Heinz join to form Kraft Heinz

2008
Consumer Goods Technology names Kraft Foods "Most Innovative Company"

NABISCO

2000
Nabisco merges with Kraft General Foods, Inc.

1969
The company makes more than $2.5 billion in sales

Mondelēz International

2012
Kraft Foods splits into Kraft Foods Group and Mondelēz International

21

Glossary

advertising—using notices and messages to announce or promote something

beverage—something you can drink

brands—categories of products all made by the same company

classic—popular for a long time due to excellence

consumption—the act of eating, drinking, or using up something

food pantries—places where people in need can get food for free

founders—the people who created a company

headquarters—a company's main offices

hurricanes—spinning rainstorms that start over warm waters

international—outside of the United States

merged—joined together to form one company

nutrients—things that are needed for healthy growth and functioning

pasteurize—to heat something to a high temperature to kill bacteria before cooling quickly

patent—an official document that says an inventor is the only person who can make or sell an invention

produce—fresh fruits, vegetables, and herbs

shelf life—the length of time food stays fresh

sponsor—a person or organization that gives money to others for a project or activity in return for being able to promote their brand

volunteers—people who do something for others without expecting money in return

warehouses—large buildings or rooms used for storing goods

whole grains—grains that have not been processed; whole grains have more nutrients than processed grains.

To Learn More

AT THE LIBRARY

Apps, Jerold W. *Casper Jaggi: Master Swiss Cheese Maker.* Madison, Wis.: Wisconsin Historical Society Press, 2008.

Green, Sara. *Kellogg's.* Minneapolis, Minn.: Bellwether Media, 2015.

Sullivan, Jaclyn. *What's In Your Macaroni and Cheese?* New York, N.Y.: PowerKids Press, 2012.

ON THE WEB

Learning more about Kraft is as easy as 1, 2, 3.

1. Go to www.factsurfer.com.

2. Enter "Kraft" into the search box.

3. Click the "Surf" button and you will see a list of related web sites.

With factsurfer.com, finding more information is just a click away.

Index